Aunt Margie's Best Italian Cooking

Copyright © 2015, 2020 by Nick & Janet Aiossa
All rights reserved.

No part of this book may be reproduced in any form or by any means, electronic or mechanical; including photocopying, recording, or by any information storage and retrieval system, without written permission from the publisher.

ISBN 10: 0-9769360-4-6
ISBN 13: 978-0-9769360-4-6

*To Margie Aiossa
for the joy her cooking brought to so many.*

*To Janet Aiossa, Margie's apprentice,
who shared her love of cooking and inspired this book.*

The Pleasure of Family & Friends

A Sharing Mindset

Grandma and Grandpa were generous, loving family people. As Italians, they believed there should always be an ample supply of good food in the house, and that there was always room to squeeze a few more people around the dinner table. Eating dinner was an unhurried pleasure and a time to thoroughly enjoy the company of others. No one believed this more than their daughter, Margie. She planned and prepared lavish meals to share with those she loved, and often times with those she met at her dinner table for the first time.

Margie, smooth and flawless in her preparation, forever intent on peeking to see the expression of her dinner guests course after course, finding great delight in the moment. She loved sharing her talents of turning fresh ingredients into a culinary masterpiece. As the host and cook, she minded the pots lining the stove, adding just the right amount of seasoning to each, letting one simmer, one boil and yet others removed to serve. There is no panic, 4 or 20, it's a pleasure to do what you love and enjoy the happiness you bring to others.

Guests continue to arrive with flowers, wine, pastries and homemade desserts. First time guests are amazed at the ease in which the meal evolves and all comes together so nicely. They are relaxed, happy and enjoying the antipastos and Margie is attentive to whatever they need. She reminds them that it's important to not fill up too quickly, there's more–much more to come.

In that spirit, enjoy all the deliciously prepared cuisine, as we have all our lives and more so as we reviewed each recipe during the production of this book. We cooked, sampled, occasionally modified measures and tested the baking and cooking times to be sure they were perfect. It's Margie's inspiration, but as with all good recipes, it's subjective and yields to personal preferences. So feel free to adjust the subtle seasonings to suit your particular taste.

Enjoy! Be sure to try all of Aunt Margie's *Best* Italian Cooking, there's so much to love.

The Aiossa Family

Aunt Margie's
Best Italian Cooking

A tribute to a great cook, 89 years in the making.

Introduction

It all began in an Italian neighborhood in Brooklyn, N.Y. Margaret Aiossa, born Margaret Rugolo in 1922 to Sebastiano and Rosa Rugolo, Italian immigrants who arrived at Ellis Island, N.Y. in 1906. They began their life in the new world with little more than old-world skills and a passion to work hard and succeed.

Margie was one of eight girls in a family of fourteen children. Years later, with families of their own, Sundays were often dinner at Grandma's house. It was so much more than a great meal. It was a Rugolo bonding experience attended by the many husbands, wives and children of the family. It never failed to be an Italian culinary extravaganza with lots of fresh, meticulously prepared, wholesome food.

Grandma Rosa stirred and tasted the pot of tomato sauce and oversaw the preparation of the other dishes as well. Grandpa Sebastiano provided the freshest of vegetables and herbs from his spectacular garden. Each meal was planned to perfection and cooked with joy. As kids we thought everyone ate like we did. The family sat in groups throughout the house and gardens for an authentic Italian dinner that was always fun and included entertainment in the form of skits, storytelling and song. Laughter and delicious food were always in abundance.

Throughout the meal, food was continually being offered. With fresh made and delicious antipastos, breads, pastas, meat dishes, cakes, cookies and desserts—no one really needed to be coaxed.

This book is a tribute to Margie, one of the best Italian cooks to emerge from a family that made Sunday dinners a cause for celebration. Always modest despite the raves and accolades she received, Margie kept it simple and always made it look easy. In the generous spirit of sharing which she was known for, we invite you to try her favorite dishes. Cooking was part of her Italian heritage, and remained her passion. No one left her table hungry and all left happy–but none happier than Aunt Margie who loved watching people enjoy eating.

Our family believes that Italian food is one of life's true pleasures and deserving of its vast popularity. We hope you enjoy Aunt Margie's delicious recipes and please be sure to share her joy with those you love!

In her memory, with pleasure,
Nick Aiossa, Margie's son

Aunt Margie's Best Italian Cooking

Table of Contents

Appetizers..1

Soups..17

Veggies & Sides...27

Main Dishes 41

Desserts..85

Appetizers

Antipasto..2

Fresh Tomato Basil Salad..3

Fried Calamari...4

Cold Octopus Salad...6

Ricotta & Pepperoni Calzone..8

Spinach Quiche...10

Tomato, Basil & Cheese Sticks..11

Artichoke Pie...12

'Pizza Fritta'–Fried Pizza Dough...14

Fresh Pizza Sauce..14

Tomato Bruschetta..15

Appetizers

Antipasto

Open the meal with appetizers you love; below are suggestions of a few of our favorites.

Ingredients

1 lb. small balls of fresh mozzarella cheese (bocconcini)
1 1/2 tbsp. extra virgin olive oil
3 tbsp. fresh basil
1 tbsp. chopped fresh flat-leaf parsley
1/2 tsp. crushed red pepper flakes
Coarse salt and freshly ground pepper
1 cup roasted red peppers, drained
1 small clove garlic, thinly sliced
2 large heads radicchio or lettuce
8 fresh figs, halved lengthwise
2 cups artichoke hearts, drained
1 lb. aged parmesan cheese, shaved
1 lb. aged asiago cheese, cubed
1 lb. aged provolone cheese, cubed
3/4 lb. capicola, thinly sliced
2 ripe beefsteak tomatoes, sliced
1 1/2 cups pepperoncini, drained
1 1/2 cups mixed olives, drained
3/4 lb. genoa salami, thinly sliced
3/4 lb. prosciutto, very thinly sliced

Directions

1. In a medium bowl, combine bocconcini, olive oil, basil, parsley, and red-pepper flakes. Season with salt and pepper; stir until all bocconcini is well covered. Set aside.

2. In a small bowl, combine roasted red peppers and thinly sliced garlic. Set aside.

3. Line a large platter with radicchio leaves.

4. Arrange ingredients on platter in a decorative pattern, keeping like ingredients together. Include ingredients that had been set aside.

Serve with breadsticks or crusty Italian bread.

Appetizers

Fresh Tomato Basil Salad

Ingredients

2-3 of each, fresh vine-ripened medium size plum and beefsteak tomatoes

3 tbsp. red wine vinegar

2 tbsp. fresh red onion, thinly sliced

6 fresh basil leaves, quartered

4 tbsp. extra virgin olive oil

1 clove garlic, minced

1/2 tsp. fresh oregano leaves, chopped

Large pinch of dried oregano

1/4 tsp. fresh squeezed lemon juice

1/4 tsp. garlic salt

Directions

1. Wash and slice tomatoes, cutting plum tomatoes in 1/4" slices and beefsteak in quarters and then again in half.

2. Place cut tomatoes in a medium bowl and add vinegar, onion, basil, olive oil, garlic, fresh and dry oregano, lemon juice, and garlic salt.

3. Gently mix ingredients together, taking care not to break tomatoes apart.

4. Let sit to marinate for 7 minutes.

Serve with crusty Italian bread for dipping.

Fried Calamari

Ingredients

1 1/2 cups extra virgin olive oil for frying
1 lb. clean squid with tentacles
2 cups flour
3 tbsp. fresh parsley, finely chopped
2 tbsp. black pepper, fresh ground
1 tsp. paprika
1/2 cup milk
2 tsp. garlic salt

Garnish

1 tsp. sea salt
2 fresh lemons, sliced into wedges
1 cup of pasta sauce (page 42)

Directions

1. Clean squid, cut body into 1/2" thick rings.
2. Mix the flour and milk in a large bowl and blend in the remaining seasoning ingredients. Start with a small batch, enough to fill frying pan.
3. In a large frying pan, heat about 1/4" layer of olive oil over medium heat.
4. Place squid into the batter and coat well. Carefully add the squid to the hot oil and fry until crisp and light golden brown, turning as necessary, cooking no more than one minute per batch. Overcooking will toughen the calamari.
5. Remove with a large slotted spoon and place the fried calamari on a paper-towel lined plate to drain excess oil.

Serve on a platter with lemon wedges and sprinkle lightly with salt. Use pasta sauce for dipping.

Appetizers

Cold Octopus Salad

Ingredients

2 lbs. fresh octopus, cleaned
3 cloves of garlic, smashed
1 cup Italian white wine
1 small red onion, sliced
3 tbsp. extra virgin olive oil
3 tbsp. fresh basil, cut
1 tsp. fresh oregano, cut
3 tbsp. fresh lemon juice
2 tbsp. fresh parsley leaves, whole
2 tbsp. lemon zest (see page 108, #2 for easy method)
1/4 tsp. crushed red pepper

Directions

1. Rinse the octopus well under running water, removing dark or shell-like pieces.

2. In a large pot, heat to a boil an ample amount of water to cover the octopus. Add the octopus and garlic and cover. Cook for 25 minutes on medium-low heat.

3. Remove half the water from the pot and add wine, 1/2 the onion and dash of red pepper and cook for an additional 20 minutes, until fork tender.

4. Remove from heat and let cool.

5. Slice octopus into 1" pieces and place in a large bowl with a cup of cooking juices. Add olive oil, remainder of onion, basil, oregano and lemon juice. Gently mix ingredients together.

6. Place finished salad on a platter, add parsley, lemon zest and a dash of crushed red pepper.

Serve with hard bread wedges to dip juices or atop crusty Italian bread slices or bed of romaine lettuce with a squeeze of fresh lemon juice.

Ricotta & Pepperoni Calzone

Ingredients

Fresh made dough (page 48) or 2 loaves of frozen bread or pizza dough

15 oz. ricotta cheese

1 1/2 cups of mozzarella, cut to 1/4" cubes

1/2 cup parmesan cheese, grated

2 eggs, well beaten

1/3 cup fresh parsley, finely chopped

2 cloves garlic, minced

Dash of black pepper

Dash crushed red pepper

6 oz. pepperoni, sliced thin

5 tbsp. extra virgin olive oil

2 cups pasta sauce (page 42)

Alternate Fillings

Spinach & ricotta

Ham or prosciutto & ricotta

Escarole & Anchovy fillets

Seedless grapes & pine nuts

Apples & provolone

Sun-dried tomatoes & ricotta

Olives & raisins

Sausage & provolone

Directions

1. Let dough rise.
2. Oil 2 large baking pans.
3. Spread dusting of flour on flat surface, roll dough out to approx. 1/4" thick.
4. Using a pie pan or any 7-9" dish as a template, cut dough in a circle to be filled.
5. In a bowl combine the filling by mixing the ricotta with cubes of mozzarella, parmesan, eggs, parsley, garlic, black pepper and crushed red pepper.
6. Place filling on half the dough circles leaving at least a 1/2" from edge. Place slices of pepperoni on top of filling mix. Add a few spoonfuls of pasta sauce.
7. Fold over to cover filling, dip fingers in warm water and wet the edges. Pinch the edges closed with a fork.
8. Brush tops with olive oil and place on cookie sheets. Cut a 1" slit in top of each calzone to serve as a vent for steam to escape.
9. Continue until pan is full of unbaked calzones.
10. Bake in pre-heated oven at 450°F for 10 to 12 minutes, until golden brown. Let cool slightly.

Serve warm with glass of burgundy wine, beer or soft drink.

Appetizers

Spinach Quiche

Ingredients

15 oz. ricotta cheese

3 eggs, beaten

12 oz. leaf spinach, uncooked or 2 packages of frozen spinach

1/2 cup parmesan cheese, grated

1/2 tsp. sea salt

Dash of black pepper

1 Pie Crust -- see page 12 for homemade recipe, or use store-bought frozen pie crust.

Directions

1. Preheat oven to 350°F
2. Mix all ingredients in large bowl.
3. Bake empty pie crust at 350°F for 5 minutes.
4. Add mixed ingredients to warmed pie crust shell.
5. Bake filled pie crust at 350°F for 45 minutes or until center does not 'jiggle' when you shake the quiche.

Serve warm with Fresh Tomato Basil Salad (page 3) or with rolled thin slices of genoa salami.

Appetizers

Tomato, Basil & Cheese Sticks

Ingredients

36 fresh vine-ripened small cherry tomatoes or smaller grape tomatoes

18 fresh basil leaves, cut in half

16 oz. small fresh mozzarella balls or 16 oz. block mozzarella

3 tbsp. extra virgin olive oil

36 toothpicks

Directions

1. Wash and dry tomatoes and basil leaves.
2. Brush basil leaves with olive oil. With a kitchen scissors, cut in half, place on plate and set aside.
3. Cut mozzarella, if block, into 36 $1/2$" cubes.
4. Pierce with toothpick in sequence: a tomato, $1/2$ basil leaf and a ball or cube of mozzarella.
5. Place Tomato, Basil & Cheese Sticks on platter.

Serve with bruschetta, or thinly sliced crusty Italian bread drizzled with extra virgin olive oil, or add to a tray of your favorite antipasto.

Artichoke Pie

Ingredients

2 12-oz. jars cut artichoke hearts

1/2 lb. thinly sliced pepperoni or genoa salami, diced

1 cup mozzarella cheese, 1/2" cubes

1/3 cup romano cheese, grated

4 eggs, well beaten

Dash of pepper

1 unbaked 9" deep dish pie shell (see ingredients/directions below) or use frozen store-bought.

Directions

1. Mix all ingredients in large bowl.
2. Bake empty pie crust at 350°F for 5 minutes.
3. Add mixed ingredients to warmed empty pie crust shell and level until even.
4. Bake at 350°F for 45 minutes, or until center is firm and doesn't 'jiggle' when you move the pan.

Pie Shell Ingredients

Makes one 9" deep dish pie crust

1 cup flour

1/4 tsp. sea salt

4 oz. cold butter, 1 stick or 1/2 cup chilled vegetable shortening

2 tbsp. ice water

Pie Shell Directions

1. Mix flour and salt in a large bowl.
2. Cut cold butter or shortening into 1/2" cubes and blend into flour mixture with a pastry cutter. Work together until there are no big clumps.
3. Add ice water and mix just until you can form dough into a ball. Do not over mix.
4. Seal in plastic wrap and chill for 1 hour.
5. Lightly flour working area and rolling pin. Roll pastry in one direction at a time, turning and lightly flouring surface to prevent crust from sticking.
6. Using your pie plate as a guide, roll until the pastry is slightly larger and about 1/8" thick.
7. Soft-fold in half and transfer to the pie plate.
8. Unfold and gently fit into the pie plate.
9. Trim off excess. Crimp rim with your fingers or a fork.

Appetizers

'Pizza Fritta' – Fried Pizza Dough

A simple and delicious snack!

Ingredients

1 lb. pizza dough

1/4 cup extra virgin olive oil

1 clove garlic, finely chopped

1 tsp. coarse salt

Fresh Pizza Sauce

28 oz. can crushed plum tomatoes

1 clove garlic, sliced

3 tbsp. extra virgin olive oil

2 tbsp. fresh basil, cut

1/4 tsp. dry oregano

1/2 tsp. sea salt

Cheese Topping

8 oz. provolone or mozzarella, shredded

3 tbsp. parmesan, grated

Directions

1. Roll dough to 1/4" thick and cut into 6" x 2" strips.
2. Heat olive oil in a deep frying pan. Sauté garlic until golden brown. Remove and set aside.
3. Taking care not to splash and burn yourself (a kitchen glove works well), drop strips of dough into the hot oil until lightly golden brown, turning to cook both sides.
4. Quickly drain on paper towel and eat hot.

Sprinkle with shredded provolone or mozzarella and grated parmesan while hot and dip in pizza sauce. Or enjoy naked-soft pretzel style, with a sprinkle of coarse salt. Delicious either way!

Tomato Bruschetta

A simple and delicious snack!

Ingredients

1 loaf crusty Italian bread

3 cloves garlic

3 large beefsteak tomatoes, 6 plum or 12 cherry tomatoes

3 tbsp. extra virgin olive oil

2 tbsp. parmesan cheese, grated

3 tbsp. fresh basil, chopped

1/2 tsp. sea salt

Directions

1. Cut loaf of bread into 1/2" slices and lightly toast.

2. Cut 2 of the 3 garlic cloves in half and rub toast slices with garlic and brush with olive oil.

3. Chop tomatoes into small pieces and combine with parmesan cheese, chopped basil, 1 minced garlic clove and salt. Mix well and place on top of bread slices.

Drizzle with additional olive oil and serve.

Soups

Rich Lentil Soup..18

Hearty Minestrone..19

Split Pea Soup..20

Pasta & Bean Soup–Pasta e Faglioli....................................22

Fresh Tomato Soup...23

Homemade Chicken Soup...24

Soups

Rich Lentil Soup

Ingredients

8 oz. bag of dry lentils

2 tsp. extra virgin olive oil

4 oz. smoked ham, diced sausage and/or ham shank bone

1 medium onion, finely chopped

2-3 ribs of celery, sliced thin

2 cloves of garlic, minced

1 large carrot, sliced thin

2 tbsp. celery leaves, chopped

32 oz. carton chicken broth

2 cups water

Dash of sea salt

Dash of black pepper

Fresh cut parsley

Directions

1. Sort and clean lentils, removing any stones and imperfections. Place lentils in large bowl in sink, fill with water and drain. Rinse again and drain.

2. Heat olive oil in large soup pot on medium heat. Brown diced meat. Add onion, celery and garlic. Sauté for 3 minutes.

3. Slowly add lentils, stirring into meat mixture.

4. Add chicken broth, ham bone, carrots, water, celery leaves, salt and pepper.

5. Cover and simmer on low heat for 45 minutes, stirring occasionally.

Serve with a garnish of parsley.

Hearty Minestrone Soup

Ingredients

3 tbsp. extra virgin olive oil
2 large cloves garlic, finely chopped
1 large onion, chopped
4 ribs celery, chopped
4 medium carrots, sliced
32 oz. carton chicken broth
2 cups water
28 oz. can crushed tomatoes
1/2 cup burgundy wine
14 oz. can kidney beans, drained
14 oz. can garbanzo beans, drained
14 oz. can green beans, drained
3 zucchinis, quartered and sliced
2 cups fresh baby spinach
1 tbsp. fresh oregano, chopped
2 tbsp. fresh basil, chopped
1/2 tsp. each salt and pepper
1 cup seashell pasta
2 tbsp. parmesan cheese, grated

Directions

1. In a large soup pot heat olive oil over low heat and sauté chopped garlic until golden color. Add chopped onion and sauté for 5 minutes. Add celery and carrots, mix well and sauté for 2 minutes.

2. Add chicken broth, water and crushed tomatoes, increase heat until boiling, stirring often. Add wine, kidney beans, garbanzo beans, green beans, zucchini, spinach, oregano, basil, salt and pepper. Reduce heat and simmer for 1 hour.

3. Cook 1 cup seashell pasta in boiling water until al dente. Add cooked pasta to soup and stir well.

Serve with a sprinkle of parmesan cheese and crusty Italian bread slices.

Split Pea Soup

Ingredients

2 tbsp. extra virgin olive oil
2 cloves garlic, minced
1 medium onion, chopped
2 medium carrots, thinly sliced
2 ribs of celery, thinly sliced
1 medium tomato, chopped
32 oz. carton chicken broth
4 cups water
1 ham hock, ham bone
2 cups dried split peas, cleaned, rinsed and drained
1 bay leaf
1 tsp. dried thyme
1/2 tsp. each salt and pepper
2 tbsp. fresh parsley, chopped

Directions

1. In a large soup pot heat olive oil over low heat and sauté minced garlic until golden color. Add chopped onion and sauté for 5 minutes. Add carrots, celery and tomato, mix well and sauté for 2 minutes.

2. Add chicken broth, water and ham hock and increase heat to boiling, stirring often. Add split peas, bay leaf and thyme. Reduce heat, cover and simmer for 1 1/2 hours or until peas are tender, stirring often.

3. Remove ham hock and when cool enough to handle, remove and shred any meat from the bone and add to the soup.

4. Season the soup with salt and pepper, add a small amount of water to thin the soup. If desired soup may be puréed in blender or food processor. Reheat and add parsley.

Serve with a garnish of fresh parsley and a light sprinkle of grated parmesan.

Pasta & Bean Soup—Pasta e Faglioli

Ingredients

- 1 thick slice boneless ham, cut into $1/2$" squares
- 2 tbsp. extra virgin olive oil
- 2 sprigs fresh rosemary, cut
- $1/2$ tsp. ground thyme
- 2 dried bay leaves
- 1 medium onion, finely chopped
- 1 carrot, quartered and sliced
- 3 sprigs parsley, chopped
- 1 rib celery, finely chopped
- 3 cloves garlic, minced
- $1/2$ tsp. sea salt
- $1/4$ tsp. black pepper, fresh ground
- 2 15-oz. cans red kidney beans or white cannolini beans
- 1 cup canned tomato sauce
- 2 cups water
- 32 oz. carton chicken broth
- $3/4$ lb. elbow or mezze penne pasta
- 3 tbsp. romano cheese, grated

Directions

1. In a large 4-quart pot on medium heat add oil and ham.
2. Brown the ham bits lightly, add herbs, chopped vegetables, and garlic. Season vegetables with salt and pepper.
3. Add beans, tomato sauce, water and chicken broth. Raise heat to high and bring soup to a rapid boil. Add pasta.
4. Reduce to medium heat and continue to cook soup, stirring occasionally for 5 to 8 minutes until pasta is cooked al dente or to taste.
5. Remove herb stems and bay leaves from soup and let soup breathe and cool for a few minutes prior to serving.

Top with grated romano cheese, a pinch of crushed red pepper and serve with crusty Italian bread for dipping.

Fresh Tomato Soup

Ingredients

3 tbsp. extra virgin olive oil
2 cloves garlic, sliced thin
2 small yellow onions, chopped
2 ribs celery, cut to 1/4" arches
1 small carrot, thin round slices
3 cups vegetable broth
10-12 medium plum or beefsteak vine ripened tomatoes (over ripe works well), cut to 1/2" cubes
1/2 cup Aunt Margie's Prepared Breadcrumbs (page 34)
3 tbsp. burgundy wine
1 1/2 tbsp. fresh oregano leaves, cut
1 chive stem, sliced 1/8" rings
3 tbsp. fresh basil leaves, cut
1 1/2 tbsp. celery leaves, chopped
1 tsp. fresh squeezed lemon juice
1/2 tsp. sea salt
1/2 tsp. black pepper, fresh ground
Pinch of crushed red pepper

Directions

1. In a large saucepan heat olive oil on medium heat and add garlic, yellow onions, celery arches, carrots and sauté for 3 minutes, taking care not to burn. Stir often.

2. Add 1 1/2 cups of broth, tomatoes and breadcrumbs and continue to cook for 5 minutes.

3. Add the other half of vegetable broth and remaining ingredients.

4. Simmer for 20 minutes on medium-low heat with lid on until thick. Stir occasionally.

5. Put soup in a food processor or blender and purée to desired creaminess.

Garnish with minced basil leaves or fresh chives and serve with hard crusty Italian bread slices.

Homemade Chicken Soup

Ingredients for Chicken Broth

3 large chicken breasts with skin and rib bones (or 1 small whole chicken)

12 cups water

1 large onion, cut into large pieces

2 ribs celery with top leaves, cut into 3" pieces

1 medium tomato cut into large pieces

1/4 cup fresh parsley with stems

1 tsp. dried ground sage

1 tsp. dried thyme

3 cubes (12 grams each) chicken bouillon

Ingredients
to add to strained Chicken Broth

3 carrots, sliced

2 ribs celery, sliced

3/4 lb. egg noodles, pastina, or short pasta of choice

Chopped parsley for garnish

For a thicker, heartier soup add 1 cup of rice, barley or quinoa to the broth and cook 30 minutes.

Directions

1. Rinse chicken and place in a large soup pot. Add water, onion, celery, tomato, parsley, sage, thyme and chicken bouillon and bring to a boil. Reduce heat, cover and simmer for 1 to 1 1/2 hours, stirring occasionally.

2. Remove from heat, take chicken breasts out with a slotted spoon and set aside.

3. Strain broth and return to soup pot.

4. Add sliced carrots and celery and simmer at least 30 minutes.

5. When chicken has cooled enough to handle, clean off skin and bones and cut meat into bite size pieces. Return chicken chunks to soup.

6. Cook egg noodles, pastina, or pasta of choice separately.

Freeze leftover soup in airtight containers for up to 4-6 months.

Serve with cooked pasta, crackers and garnish with freshly chopped parsley.

Veggies & Sides

Zucchini Tomato Medley..28

Grandpa's Pickled Eggplant..30

Fresh Garlic Roasted Tomatoes..31

Cheesy Spinach Casserole..32

Pan Fried Escarole..33

Aunt Margie's Stuffed Artichokes..34

Aunt Margie's Prepared Breadcrumbs...34

Zucchini Casserole..36

Olive Oil Roasted Potatoes..38

Potato Croquettes...39

Zucchini Tomato Medley

Ingredients

1 large beefsteak tomato

1 tbsp. red onion, chopped or thinly sliced

1 large or 2 medium zucchinis

3 tsp. extra virgin olive oil

1 cup mozzarella, shredded

1/4 cup parmesan cheese, grated

8 fresh basil leaves, torn into quarters

Directions

1. Preheat oven to 375°F.

2. Spray bottom of a ceramic baking dish with olive oil. Cut tomato into thin slices, overlap in a single layer.

3. Sprinkle onion and basil on top of tomatoes.

4. Thinly slice zucchini and arrange a layer on top of tomatoes, overlapping slices to fit baking dish.

5. Spread mozzarella and parmesan cheeses evenly on top.

6. Drizzle with olive oil.

7. Bake uncovered 30 minutes until top is golden brown.

Let sit for 5 minutes before serving.

Grandpa's Pickled Eggplant

Ingredients
for cooking

1 lb. eggplant
1 1/2 tsp. sea salt
2 cups water
1 cup white vinegar

Ingredients
for pickling

1/2 cup extra virgin olive oil
1/2 cup red wine vinegar
6 cloves of garlic, halved
1/2 tsp. sea salt
3-4 dry bay leaves
1 tsp. dried basil
1/2 tsp. dried oregano
1 tsp. black pepper

Eggplant Selecton Tip:
Choose deep dark purple/black eggplant that is lighter in weight than others of comparable size, which is usually indicative of an eggplant with less seeds.

Directions

1. Cut unpeeled eggplant in 1/2" slices and place in saucepan. Sprinkle with sea salt.

2. Cover the eggplant with water and vinegar. If eggplant isn't covered, add additional 2 cups water to 1 cup vinegar.

3. Cover and heat until boiling. Reduce heat and simmer for 5 minutes. Remove from heat, drain and let cool. Fully drain and carefully squeeze out excess liquid.

4. In large bowl with pouring spout, mix olive oil, wine vinegar, basil, oregano, salt and pepper. Pour 1/2" of pickling mixture to the bottom of a 24-32 oz. jar with a lid. Add a layer of cooked eggplant, 2-3 halved cloves of garlic and 2 ripped halves of bay leaves on top of eggplant. Repeat layering of pickling mixture, eggplant, garlic and bay leaves until all eggplant is jarred.

5. Place pickled eggplant in refrigerator for 2-3 days. Turn occasionally to keep liquid and spices well mixed.

Enjoy with sesame bread sticks, or as a side dish.

Fresh Garlic Roasted Tomatoes

Ingredients

3 lbs. vine ripened plum tomatoes, split in half long ways, or fresh cherry tomatoes, whole

6 tbsp. extra virgin olive oil

3 tbsp. balsamic vinegar

2 tbsp. fresh lemon juice

3 tbsp. parsley leaves, chopped

2 tbsp. fresh oregano leaves, cut

3 sprigs fresh rosemary, chopped

2 tbsp. fresh basil leaves, cut

6 cloves of garlic, sliced very thin

Directions

1. In a large ceramic baking pan place tomatoes in a single layer. Drizzle olive oil, vinegar and lemon juice.

2. Sprinkle garlic and herbs over the tomatoes as evenly as possible.

3. Bake at 200°F for approximately 2 hours, stir once after 1 hour to assure even roasting. Add more olive oil and vinegar if necessary. Do not let tomatoes dry out.

Serve as a veggie side, or atop slices of crusty Italian bread with cooked liquid from pan as drizzle.

Cheesy Spinach Casserole

Ingredients

1 1/2 cups ricotta cheese

1/4 cup parsley, finely chopped

3 eggs, beaten

4 tbsp. butter, cut into large chunks

1/4 lb. aged provolone cheese, cut into small chunks

1/4 cup parmesan, grated

2 packages frozen chopped spinach, thawed and drained

3 tbsp. flour

4 cherry or 2 plum tomatoes

Directions

1. Place first six ingredients in a large bowl and mix well.
2. Add thawed, drained spinach and flour. Blend well.
3. Spray ceramic baking dish with olive oil. Pour mixture in and top with thinly sliced cherry or plum tomatoes.
4. Bake uncovered at 350°F for 1 hour. Serve warm.

Pan Fried Escarole

Ingredients

1 head escarole or rapini
1 rib celery, thinly sliced
1 clove garlic, whole
3 tbsp. extra virgin olive oil
1 clove garlic, sliced
2 tbsp. pine nuts, whole
1/2 tsp. garlic salt
1/4 tsp. crushed red pepper

Directions

1. Rinse escarole or rapini (broccoli rabe) well, leaf by leaf and place in large covered saucepan.

2. Add 1/2 cup water and bring to a boil. Reduce heat, cover and steam escarole with celery and 1 clove of garlic for 10 minutes until tender.

3. Drain in colander and squeeze out excess liquid.

4. Heat olive oil in skillet on medium heat and brown clove of sliced garlic and pine nuts until golden.

5. Add escarole, celery, garlic salt and crushed red pepper and cook for 3 minutes, stirring occasionally.

Serve warm or cold as a veggie side. Also delicious eaten as a sandwich with capicola or as filling for calzone.

Aunt Margie's Stuffed Artichokes

Ingredients

4 large fresh artichokes
4-6 tsp. extra virgin olive oil
2 cups Aunt Margie's Prepared Breadcrumbs (see below)

Aunt Margie's Prepared Breadcrumbs

- 2 cups of hard dried bread, ground in food processor or blender until fine crumbs, or 2 cups store bought Italian breadcrumbs
- 1/3 cup of grated parmesan or romano cheese
- 1/2 cup of finely chopped fresh parsley
- 1/2 tsp. garlic powder

Mix all ingredients thoroughly.
Leftover prepared breadcrumbs can be stored in a sealed container in the freezer.

Directions

1. Rinse artichokes. With a sharp knife, cut each stem to approximately 1". Trim all petal leaf tips with a kitchen scissors.

2. Spread petals to open artichoke. With a spoon, fill the petals of each artichoke with prepared breadcrumbs (1/2 tsp. to full tsp), pushing petals open as you go. Depending on size, allow up to 3/4 cup of breadcrumbs per artichoke.

3. Place artichokes, stem down, in a dutch oven or deep skillet with lid in 3/4" of water.

4. Drizzle 1+ tsp. of olive oil on top of each breadcrumb stuffed artichoke.

5. Cover and heat to boiling. Reduce heat and simmer for 1 hour, checking periodically to see that water level remains at 1/2" minimum. Add water as needed.

6. After an hour test a petal for tenderness. If not tender, cook an additional 15-30 minutes.

Serve warm as a side dish for fish or meat.

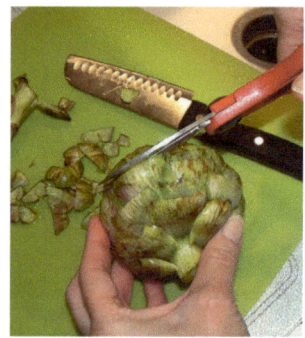

Zucchini Casserole

Ingredients

3/4 cups flour
1 1/2 tsp. baking powder
1/2 tsp. sea salt
1/2 tsp. black pepper
1/2 tsp. crushed red pepper
4 medium zucchini, diced
2 1/2 cups sharp cheddar, shredded
1 tbsp. fresh oregano, finely chopped
1 tbsp. fresh basil, finely chopped
1 medium onion, finely chopped
3/4 cup ham or canadian bacon, diced
4 large eggs
1/3 cup extra virgin olive oil
1/4 cup romano cheese, grated

Directions

1. Preheat oven to 350°F.
2. Mix flour, baking powder and salt together.
3. Slice 12 very thin slices of zucchini and set aside. Chop remaining zucchini into 1/2" cubes and place into large mixing bowl.
4. Add 1 cup of shredded cheddar cheese, flour mixture, chopped onion, basil, oregano and ham.
5. Whisk eggs in a separate bowl with olive oil.
6. Add black and red pepper. Mix all ingredients and place in an olive oil sprayed casserole dish.
7. Place 12 thin slices of zucchini on top and sprinkle with remaining 1/2 cup of cheddar cheese and 1/4 cup romano cheese.
8. Bake at 350°F for 45 minutes.

Serve warm. Top with pasta sauce or sprinkle with grated romano cheese.

Veggies & Sides

Olive Oil Roasted Potatoes

Ingredients

8 medium russet potatoes
1/2 cup extra virgin olive oil
4 small yellow onions
6 cloves garlic, halved
1/2 tsp. dried oregano
1/2 tsp. dried thyme
1/4 tsp. sea salt
1/8 tsp. black pepper, fresh ground
2 sprigs fresh rosemary

Directions

1. Wash, dry, and peel potatoes. Slice each potato into quarters and place in large bowl with olive oil.

2. Peel, quarter and separate layers of all 4 onions. Add to the potatoes with garlic, oregano, thyme, salt and pepper.

3. Gently mix all ingredients together.

4. Pour potato mixture into a ceramic baking dish.

5. Bake at 375°F for 30 minutes, stirring and turning potatoes every 10 minutes. Broil for an additional 10-15 minutes until lightly golden brown.

Garnish with fresh rosemary. Enjoy with beef or pork roasts, fish or makes a great side for our famous Lemon Roasted Chicken (page 60).

Potato Croquettes

Ingredients

¼ cup extra virgin olive oil

4-6 large potatoes, peeled and cubed

4 eggs, beaten

½ cup cooked ham, ¼" cubes

½ cup parmesan cheese, grated

½ cup aged provolone, shredded

½ tsp. sea salt

½ tsp. black pepper, fresh ground

¼ tsp. crushed red pepper

Coating

2 eggs, beaten

½ cup whole milk

1 cup flour

1 cup Aunt Margie's Prepared Breadcrumbs (see page 34)

Directions

1. Boil the potatoes in salted water until tender. Drain. Cool.

2. In a large bowl mash potatoes, leaving some lumps. Stir in 4 eggs, ham, and cheeses and mix well. Season with salt and peppers.

3. Put flour on a large plate, and breadcrumbs on another large plate. Whisk 2 eggs with milk in a large bowl.

4. With your hands, form a 3" log (put flour on your hands to avoid sticking). Coat the croquette log in flour, then the egg mixture, and lastly, the breadcrumbs. Continue until all potato mixture is finished.

5. Heat oil in a large skillet on medium heat. Protect yourself from hot oil splashing.

6. Carefully place several croquettes in the hot oil and fry until golden brown. Turn to brown each side. Remove, drain and cool on paper towels. Continue until all croquettes are done.

Serve warm with fresh tomato.

Main Dishes

Aunt Margie's Legendary Meatballs..42

Pasta Sauce..42

Homemade Manicotti...44

Sicilian Pan Pizza..46

Neapolitan Pizza...48

Homemade Pizza Dough..48

Aunt Margie's Rolled Steak Braciole..50

Sausage & Provolone Rolls...52

Spinach & Ricotta Rolls..52

Aunt Margie's Eggplant Parmesan...54

Chicken Parmesan..56

Baked Steak Pizzaiola...58

Cheesy Lasagne..59

Lemon Roasted Chicken..60

Chicken Cacciatore...62

Savory Beef Burgundy Stew...64

Bacon Wrapped Pork Roast...66

Veal Marsala...68

Stuffed Bell Peppers...70

Flaky Breaded Salmon..72

Shrimp Scampi...74

Linguine with Clam Sauce...76

Spaghetti with Ricotta & Tomato..78

Mussels in Wine Sauce...79

Blue Claw Crab Sauce..80

Fresh Spinach and Clams...82

Aunt Margie's Meatloaf Siciliano...83

Main Dishes

Aunt Margie's Legendary Meatballs

Ingredients

2 lbs. ground sirloin
1/4 loaf Italian bread
2 large eggs
1 cup Aunt Margie's Prepared Breadcrumbs (page 34)
3/4 cup romano cheese, grated
2/3 cup parsley, finely chopped
2 cloves fresh garlic, minced or 2 tsp. garlic powder
1/2 tsp. black pepper

Directions

1. Soak bread in water and squeeze out excess. Thoroughly mix all ingredients with hands or with bread dough attachment of electric mixer. Place in an airtight container and let marinate overnight in refrigerator.

3. Form meatballs to 2" balls, or any size of your choice.

4. Heat a thin layer of olive oil in a large frying pan. Pan needs to be medium hot to seal meat. Fry meatballs, turning often until all sides are brown. Meatballs will have a pink center, but will fully cook in the sauce. Place browned meatballs on paper towels to drain excess oil. May also be baked on cookie sheets at 350° for 30 minutes, turning occasionally to brown all sides.

5. Prepare pasta sauce (recipe below), add meatballs and simmer on low for 2-3 hours. Stir occasionally and gently, so as not to break apart meatballs. For added flavor, pan fried sausage and/or chunks of pork may also be added to cook with the sauce.

Serve over your favorite pasta.

Pasta Sauce Ingredients

3 cloves of garlic
2 tbsp. extra virgin olive oil
105 oz. can of crushed tomatoes
1/8 tsp. sea salt and black pepper
Pinch of crushed red pepper
8 fresh basil leaves, chopped
2 tsp. fresh oregano, chopped
1/3 cup burgundy wine
4 dried bay leaves
1/2 cup parmesan cheese, grated

Pasta Sauce Directions

1. Coat a large pot with olive oil and sauté 3 cloves of garlic until golden brown.

2. Add balance of ingredients, cover and simmer on low heat for 2-3 hours, stirring occasionally so as not to burn bottom.

Main Dishes

Homemade Manicotti

Ingredients *for Crepes*

3 eggs
2 tbsp. melted butter
1 1/4 cups flour
1 1/2 cups of milk
1/8 tsp. sea salt
4 cups pasta sauce (page 42)

Ingredients *for Cheese Filling*

15 oz. ricotta cheese
1 1/2 cups of mozzarella,
 cut to 1/4" cubes
1/2 cup parmesan cheese, grated
2 eggs, well beaten
1/3 cup fresh parsley, finely chopped
Dash of black pepper

Cheese filling can also be used for:
Stuffed Shells
Baked Ziti
Lasagne
Calzone
Ricotta Rolls

Directions *for Crepes*

1. Whisk eggs and melted butter in a mixing bowl. Gradually add flour, milk and salt and whisk until smooth. Batter consistency should be thin.

2. Spray olive oil on small frying pan and heat to medium high.

3. Pour a couple spoonfuls of batter and immediately rotate pan slightly to spread crepe evenly in a circle.

4. Cook each side lightly for 10-15 seconds. Crepes should be almost white, not golden brown.

5. Stack crepes and set aside for filling.

Directions *for Baking*

1. Preheat oven to 350°F. Line baking dish with 3/4 cup of pasta sauce. Spread to cover bottom of dish.

2. On a plate, place a crepe and spoon two tbsp. of cheese filling in the center. Place one end over middle filling and roll up.

3. Place seam-side down in prepared baking dish. Continue with balance of crepes.

4. Top the crepes with balance of pasta sauce and sprinkle with grated parmesan cheese.

5. Bake uncovered at 350°F for 30-45 minutes until sauce is bubbly and crepes are heated through. Let stand for 3 minutes to cool and set.

Garnish with chopped parsley and serve.

Main Dishes

45

Sicilian Pan Pizza

Ingredients

Fresh made dough (see page 48) or 2 loaves of frozen bread or pizza dough

28 oz. can whole plum tomatoes

8 tbsp. virgin olive oil, divided

2 tbsp. fresh basil leaves, cut

1/4 tsp. black pepper

1/2 tsp. crushed red pepper

1 tsp. dried oregano

1/2 cup parmesan cheese, grated

12 oz. mozzarella cheese, shredded

1 thinly sliced beefsteak tomato

This is a pizza with cheese and fresh tomato topping.
Get daring–add *your* favorite topping!

Suggested toppings
Fresh cut basil leaves
Thinly sliced pepperoni
Crumbled pre-cooked sausage
Sliced black olives
Sliced mushrooms
Sliced onions

Directions

1. Let dough rise.
2. Coat two large baking pans with 2 tbsp. olive oil.
3. Spread dusting of flour on flat surface. Roll each loaf of dough out to approximately 1/2" thickness.
4. Place dough in both pans, and with fingers slightly coated with oil, push dough out to the pan edges.
5. Place the peeled plum tomatoes in a medium bowl and with your hands, squeeze to break up the whole tomatoes until no large chunks remain.
6. Add 4 tbsp. olive oil, basil, black and crushed red pepper and oregano and mix together thoroughly.
7. Brush remaining 2 tbsp. of olive oil over the uncooked pizza dough in the pans.
8. Spoon the prepared tomato sauce on top. Place slices of tomatoes, sprinkle the parmesan cheese and add a generous amount of mozzarella cheese to both pizzas.
9. Bake in a pre-heated oven at 400°F for 15-20 minutes until the crust is a rich golden brown.
10. Remove from oven and let cool for a few minutes.

Slice with kitchen scissors or pizza cutter and serve warm.

For leftover dough, see our delicious recipe for 'Pizza Fritta' on page 14.

Main Dishes

Neapolitan Pizza

Ingredients for Pizza Dough
4 cups flour
1 envelope dry yeast (1/4 oz.)
1 tsp. sea salt
3/4 cups water
3/4 cups milk
1/8 cup extra virgin olive oil

Note: Frozen bread dough may be substituted for homemade dough. Completely thaw 2 loaves and follow directions 7-11.

Ingredients for Pizza Sauce
28 oz. can whole plum tomatoes
1/4 cup parmesan cheese, grated
2 tsp. dried oregano
1/2 tsp. garlic powder
2 tbsp. extra virgin olive oil
Dash black pepper
Dash of crushed red pepper

Cheese Pizza Topping
3 cups mozzarella cheese, shredded

Suggested toppings
Fresh cut basil leaves
Thinly sliced pepperoni
Crumbled pre-cooked sausage
Sliced black olives, mushrooms or onions
Thin sliced pineapple and ham

Directions
1. Combine 1 1/2 cups of flour, undissolved yeast and salt in a large bowl.
2. Heat water, milk and oil to 120-130°F (very warm).
3. Gradually add heated liquid to flour mixture. Beat with electric mixer 2 minutes at high speed, scraping bowl.
4. With a sturdy wooden spoon, stir in balance of flour to make a soft dough.
5. Spread a light layer of flour on a smooth surface and knead dough until smooth, about 6 minutes.
6. Cover dough with damp linen cloth for 10 minutes.
7. Divide dough into two balls and place each on oiled pizza pan or shallow baking pan. Spray top of dough with olive oil and cover top of pan with plastic wrap. Let rise in warm place until doubled in size, about 30-60 minutes.
8. When dough has risen, with lightly oiled fingers, starting from center of dough, gently press dough to the edges of pans. Re-cover with plastic wrap.
9. To prepare pizza sauce, place can of whole plum tomatoes in a blender and mix just until big pieces have been cut up. Pour tomatoes into a mixing bowl and add parmesan cheese, oregano, garlic powder, olive oil and black and red pepper. Mix thoroughly and set aside.
10. Preheat oven to 350°F. Remove plastic wrap and bake pizza dough for 10 minutes.
11. Remove from oven. Top with prepared pizza sauce, cheese and preferred toppings. Bake an additional 20 minutes or until cheese is bubbling and crust is a light golden brown.

Slice with kitchen scissors or pizza cutter and serve warm.

Main Dishes

Aunt Margie's Rolled Steak Braciole

Ingredients

2 lbs. thin-sliced steak, choose round, flank or chuck steak

3/4 cup Aunt Margie's Prepared Breadcrumbs (page 34)

4 tbsp. romano cheese, grated

3/4 cup mozzarella, shredded

2 eggs, beaten

2 cups pasta sauce (page 42)

6 tbsp. extra virgin olive oil

2 cloves garlic, minced

1/4 cup parsley, chopped

Dash sea salt and pepper

Pinch crushed red pepper

Alternate stuffings

Sliced hard boiled eggs

Sliced black olives

Raisins, soaked and plumped

Directions

1. Place steak between 2 hard plastic cutting sheets or into a large plastic freezer bag and pound and flatten using a heavy meat mallet.
2. Cut flattened steak into 6" squares.
3. Spoon beaten eggs over meat and add 1 tbsp. breadcrumbs, 1/2 tsp. romano cheese, 1 tbsp. mozzarella cheese, 1/4 clove minced garlic, 1 tsp. chopped parsley, dash salt and pepper. Braciole can also be stuffed with sliced hard boiled eggs, black olives or raisins.
4. Prepare remaining steak squares with same coatings and roll up tightly with kitchen twine, small metal skewers or toothpicks.
5. Brown meat rolls in olive oil lined skillet with lid.
6. Can be cooked with homemade pasta sauce, as you would meatballs. Or continue with braciole cooked separately adding pasta sauce to top of meat. Stir gently.
7. Cover and let simmer 2-3 hours, or until tender.

Serve sliced with sticks of 'pizza fritta', points of crusty Italian bread, or over your favorite pasta.

Main Dishes

Sausage & Provolone Rolls

Ingredients

Fresh made dough (see page 48) or 2 loaves of frozen bread dough

4 tbsp. extra virgin olive oil

2 lbs. Italian sausage

1 lb. aged provolone cheese, cut into 1/4" cubes

4 tbsp. parmesan cheese, grated

1/4 cup parsley, chopped

2 cloves garlic, minced

1 tsp. ground black pepper

Directions

1. Let dough rise.
2. Oil 2 large shallow baking pans.
3. Spread dusting of flour on flat surface, roll dough out to 1/8" thick and cut 8" x 6" rectangles to be filled.
4. Remove casing from sausage and crumble in hot skillet. Fry sausage till cooked. Drain off excess fat.
5. Spoon sausage meat onto rectangles, spreading to a half-inch from edge of cut dough.
6. Cut provolone into 1/4 inch cubes and sprinkle 8-10 cubes on top of cooked sausage. Sprinkle with parmesan, parsley, garlic, and dash of black pepper.
7. Roll filled dough pockets from bottom to top and pinch the sides closed. Prick holes in tops with fork.
8. Place unbaked rolls on baking pans, seam side down, and bake at 350°F for 30 min. or until lightly golden brown.

Alternate filling

Spinach & Ricotta Rolls

1 small onion, chopped

4 tbsp. extra virgin olive oil

2 12-oz. packages frozen spinach, thawed and drained

15 oz. ricotta cheese

1 oz. anchovies (1/2 tin)

1/4 cup parsley, chopped

1 egg, well beaten

1/4 cup parmesan cheese, grated

2 cloves garlic, minced

1/2 lb. aged provolone, cut into 1/4" cubes

Directions for Spinach & Ricotta Rolls

1. Brown onion in olive oil and add spinach. Mix well.
2. In large bowl mix ricotta with balance of ingredients.
3. Spread a layer of onion/spinach mixture and top with cheese mixture. Continue with directions 7 & 8 above.

Main Dishes

53

Aunt Margie's Eggplant Parmesan

Ingredients

- 1 eggplant, about 1 lb.
- 3 tbsp. sea salt
- 2 eggs, beaten
- 1 tsp. garlic salt
- 2 cups Aunt Margie's Prepared Breadcrumbs (page 34)
- 1/4 cup extra virgin olive oil
- 4 cups pasta sauce (page 42)
- 1 lb. mozzarella cheese, shredded
- 1/2 cup parmesan cheese, grated
- 2 tbsp. fresh basil, finely chopped
- 2 tbsp. fresh oregano, finely chopped
- Dash black pepper
- Dash crushed red pepper

Directions

1. Wash eggplant and leaving skin on, cut 1/4" thick round slices. Fill a tall bowl large enough to fit all slices with water and dissolve 3 tbsp. of sea salt. Submerge eggplant slices to soak in salted water for 1 hour, maximum overnight. Add dish with a weight on top to keep eggplant submerged in salted water. Soaking will reduce any bitterness in the eggplant.

2. Drain, rinse and pat eggplant slices dry with paper towel.

3. Whisk eggs and garlic salt in medium size bowl.

4. Place breadcrumbs in another medium size bowl.

5. Dip each slice of eggplant in egg mixture and then coat with breadcrumb mixture.

6. At this point you can either bake or fry the slices.

BAKED: Spray a cookie sheet with olive oil and fill with a single layer of eggplant slices. Drizzle a little olive oil over slices. Bake at 350°F for 20 minutes, turning once after 10 minutes until golden brown.

FRIED: Fry in extra virgin olive oil, heated on medium heat, turning once until golden brown. Place cooked slices on paper-towel lined plate to drain excess oil.

Directions for baking:

1. Preheat oven to 350°F. Spray bottom and sides of a large ceramic baking dish with olive oil.

2. Spoon a thin layer of pasta sauce on the bottom and then place a layer of cooked eggplant slices. Add a layer of shredded mozzarella, grated parmesan, dash of black pepper, dash of crushed red pepper and a sprinkle of basil and oregano. Cover with the next layer of pasta sauce, eggplant, cheeses and herbs until remaining eggplant is finished. Top layer should be covered with sauce, cheeses and herbs.

3. Bake at 350°F for 30-40 minutes or until edges are bubbling and center is hot. Let stand 10 minutes before serving.

Serve topped with pasta sauce and sprinkle of parmesan cheese. Place on Italian bread sliced toast rubbed with garlic and drizzled with olive oil, or as a side with your favorite pasta.

Main Dishes

Chicken Parmesan

Ingredients

6 thin sliced chicken cutlets, about 1 lb.

2 eggs, beaten

2 cups Aunt Margie's Prepared Breadcrumbs (page 34)

1/4 cup extra virgin olive oil

4 cups pasta sauce (page 42)

1 lb. mozzarella cheese, shredded

1/2 cup parmesan cheese, grated

2 tbsp. fresh basil, finely chopped

2 tbsp. fresh oregano, finely chopped

Dash of black pepper

Dash of garlic salt

Dash of crushed red pepper

Directions

1. Pound each chicken cutlet with kitchen mallet to thin and tenderize.

2. Dip each chicken cutlet in egg and coat both sides with prepared breadcrumbs.

3. At this point you can either bake or fry the breaded cutlets.

BAKED: Spray a rectangular baking pan with oil and fill with a single layer of cutlets. Drizzle a little olive oil on top. Bake at 350°F for 20-25 minutes until golden brown.

FRIED: Fry in olive oil, heated on medium heat, turning once until golden brown. Place cooked cutlets on paper-towel lined plate to drain excess oil.

Directions for baking:

1. Preheat oven to 350°F. Spray bottom and sides of a large ceramic baking dish with olive oil.

2. Spoon a thin layer of pasta sauce on the bottom and then place a layer of cutlets. Spoon pasta sauce over cutlets. Add a layer of shredded mozzarella, grated parmesan, dash of black pepper, dash of crushed red pepper and a sprinkle of basil and oregano. Cutlets can be baked in a single layer or if preferred, make another layer of sauce, cutlets, cheeses and herbs until all cutlets are finished. Top layer should be covered with sauce, cheeses and herbs.

3. Bake at 350°F for 25-30 minutes or until edges are bubbling and center is hot.
Let stand 10 minutes before serving.

Serve with your favorite pasta, side salad and slices of crusty Italian bread rubbed with garlic and drizzled with olive oil.

Main Dishes

Baked Steak Pizzaiola

Ingredients

- 2 lbs. chuck, round or flank steak
- 3 cloves garlic, minced
- 4 tbsp. extra virgin olive oil
- Sprinkle of dried oregano
- Sprinkle of sea salt
- 1/2 tsp. crushed red pepper
- 1 medium onion, finely chopped
- 1 tbsp. fresh basil, cut
- 1/2 tsp. dried rosemary
- 2 1/2 cups pasta sauce (page 42)
- 14 oz. can diced tomatoes
- 6 oz. fresh or canned mushrooms, sliced
- 4 medium carrots, thinly sliced
- 3 medium potatoes, halved

Directions

1. Wash and pat dry steaks and cut into individual serving sizes. Pound steaks with kitchen mallet to tenderize. Rub both sides with black pepper, crushed red pepper and salt.

2. In a large skillet, sauté 3 cloves of garlic in 2 tbsp. of olive oil until golden. Remove garlic, set aside.

3. Heat garlic-flavored oil on medium heat, browning steaks on both sides. Set aside.

4. Add additional 2 tbsp. of olive oil to pan and sauté onion with sliced fresh mushrooms until golden brown. Add pasta sauce, diced tomatoes and garlic that had been set aside and mix thoroughly with onions and mushrooms.

5. Spoon a thin layer of prepared sauce in bottom of large ceramic baking dish with lid. Place steaks on top.

6. Add carrots and potatoes and cover steaks with remaining pasta sauce, oregano, basil and rosemary.

7. Cover, bake 1 hour at 350°F. Remove from oven, stir, re-cover and bake an additional hour or until fork tender.

Let sit 7 minutes before serving.

Cheesy Lasagne

Ingredients

4 cups pasta sauce (page 42)
12 dry lasagne noodles
1/2 cup parmesan cheese, grated

Cheese Filling

15 oz. ricotta cheese
1 1/2 cups of mozzarella, cut to 1/4" cubes
1/2 cup parmesan cheese, grated
2 eggs, well beaten
1/3 cup fresh parsley, finely chopped
Dash black pepper

Directions

1. Add a tsp. of sea salt and a tbsp. of olive oil to a large pot of water and bring to a boil. Add lasagne noodles and cook for 5 minutes. Drain. Lay noodles flat on clean linen towels.
2. Mix ingredients for cheese filling.
3. Prepare a 9" x 13" baking dish with a light coating of olive oil spray. Spread 1 cup of pasta sauce on bottom.
4. Layer lasagne noodles, 1/2 of cheese filling and 1 1/4 cups of pasta sauce. Repeat. Top with remaining lasagne noodles and sauce. Sprinkle parmesan cheese over top.
5. Bake in a preheated oven at 375°F for 40-45 minutes.

Let stand and settle 7 minutes before serving.

Lemon Roasted Chicken

Ingredients

- ½ cup virgin olive oil, divided
- 1 whole bulb of garlic
- 3 tbsp. fresh garlic, chopped
- ⅓ cup Italian white wine
- ¼ cup fresh lemon juice
- 1 tsp. fresh oregano, chopped
- ½ tsp. dried oregano
- 3 sprigs fresh rosemary
- 1 tsp. fresh thyme leaves
- 1 small onion, quartered
- ½ tsp. sea salt
- ½ tsp. ground black pepper
- ¼ tsp. crushed red pepper
- 4 chicken breasts, bone-in with skin or 4 thigh/drumstick pieces or 1 whole cut up
- 2 fresh lemons (1 for zest)
- ¼ tsp. coarse salt

Directions

1. Heat ¼ cup of olive oil in a small saucepan on medium heat. Add the garlic for just 1 minute so that the garlic remains white.
2. Remove from heat and add the white wine, lemon juice, zest from one lemon (see page 108, #2 for easy zest method), oregano, rosemary, thyme, quartered onion broken apart, and ½ tsp. salt and pepper.
3. Preheat oven to 375°F.
4. Pour wine, lemon juice and seasoning mixture into a 10" x 14" ceramic baking pan.
5. Dry the chicken pieces and place them skin side up over the juice mixture.
6. Brush the chicken with remaining olive oil and shake on salt, black pepper and crushed red pepper.
7. Cut the bulb of garlic and lemons w/and w/o rind, in 1/8" slices and place them over the pieces of chicken.
8. Bake uncovered at 375°F for 40 minutes, until the chicken skin is lightly browned. For browner chicken cook on broil for an additional 2 minutes.
9. Remove from oven and cover pan with lid or aluminum foil for 10 full minutes.
10. Sprinkle with coarse salt. Serve chicken hot, covered with lemon garlic pan juices.

Serve with a side of Olive Oil Roasted Potatoes (page 38). Slice crusty Italian bread for dipping in lemon sauce.

Main Dishes

61

Chicken Cacciatore

Ingredients

4 chicken breasts with skin

4 chicken thighs with skin

2 tbsp. fresh lemon juice

1/2 cup flour

1 tsp. sea salt

1 tsp. black pepper, fresh ground

6 tbsp. extra virgin olive oil

1 red bell pepper, chopped

1 medium onion, finely chopped

3 garlic cloves, minced

3/4 cup Italian white wine

28 oz. can diced tomatoes

3/4 cup chicken broth

3 tbsp. capers, drained

1/2 tsp. dry basil

1/2 tsp. dry oregano

1/8 cup fresh oregano leaves

1/4 cup fresh basil leaves, chopped

1 tsp. romano cheese, grated

1/2 tsp. crushed red pepper

Directions

1. Brush chicken pieces with lemon juice.

2. In a large zippered plastic bag, place flour, salt and pepper, seal and shake bag to mix. Place 2-3 pieces of chicken at a time in the bag, shake gently until lightly coated with the flour mixture.

3. In a large skillet, heat the oil on medium heat.

4. Add the chicken pieces to the skillet and sauté until brown, approximately 5 minutes per side.

5. Remove the chicken and set aside.

6. Add the bell pepper, onion and garlic to the same pan and sauté over medium heat for about 5 minutes.

7. Add the wine and simmer for about 3 minutes.

8. Add the diced tomatoes and their juice, chicken broth, capers, dry basil and dry oregano. Hold fresh basil and oregano for garnish topping just prior to serving.

9. Return the chicken pieces to the skillet and immerse them in the sauce. Bring the sauce to a boil. Cover, reduce heat to medium low and continue simmering until the chicken is thoroughly cooked through, about 25-30 minutes.

10. Place the chicken on a platter. Cook the sauce for an additional 3 minutes, until it thickens slightly. Stir the sauce well and spoon it over the chicken. Sprinkle with fresh basil, fresh oregano, a light dusting of romano cheese and crushed red pepper to taste.

Serve with crusty Italian bread or hot 'Pizza Fritta' (page 14) sprinkled with parmesan cheese.

Main Dishes

Savory Beef Burgundy Stew

Ingredients

¼ cup extra virgin olive oil

½ cup flour

½ tsp. sea salt

½ tsp. black pepper

2 lbs. beef for stew, cubed

1 large onion, quartered

2 cups water

½ tsp. dried rosemary

¼ tsp. dried oregano

½ tsp. dried basil

2 tbsp. fresh parsley, chopped

Pinch crushed red pepper

2 tsp. gravy browning sauce

¼ cup burgundy wine

3 med. carrots, cut into 1" pieces

3 large potatoes, cut into bite size pieces

1 cup fresh green beans, cut into 1" pieces or one 14 oz. can cut green beans

Directions

1. In a dutch oven or large pot with lid, heat olive oil on medium high.

2. Mix flour, salt and pepper in a large zippered plastic bag. Place beef cubes in bag and shake until well coated.

3. Lightly brown onion in heated oil. Add beef and brown until seared on all sides.

4. Add water, rosemary, oregano, basil and 1 tbsp. parsley, crushed red pepper, gravy browning sauce and burgundy wine. Bring to a boil, cover and reduce heat to low.

5. Simmer on low for 2 hours, stirring occasionally. Add small amounts of water if needed. Meat should be halfway covered with liquid at all times.

6. Add carrots, potatoes and green beans. Add a small amount of water if needed, bring to a boil and then simmer on medium low for 15-20 minutes, until vegetables are soft.

Serve over steamed rice or with crusty Italian bread.

Main Dishes

65

Bacon Wrapped Pork Roast

Ingredients

1 boneless pork loin, approx. 3 lbs.
8 oz. bacon strips, uncooked
2 bulbs fresh garlic, halved
3 sprigs fresh rosemary

Meat Rub

3 cloves garlic, smashed
4 tsp. fresh rosemary, chopped
3 tsp. fresh oregano, chopped
1 tsp. garlic salt
1/2 tsp. coarse salt
1 tbsp. extra virgin olive oil
1 tbsp. fresh lemon juice
1/2 tsp. black pepper

Directions

1. In a small bowl mix all ingredients into a meat rub.
2. Place pork loin in a large ceramic baking pan and thoroughly rub with halved garlic bulbs, then meat rub mixture.
3. Wrap bacon strips around roast, securing with toothpicks. Place roast fat side down in bake pan.
4. Bake in preheated oven at 425°F for 30 minutes, turn roast over and continue to bake for an additional 30 minutes or until internal temperature reaches 145°F.
5. Remove and let sit for 3 minutes. Place on platter and slice to preferred thickness. Pour pan juices over roast and garnish with rosemary sprigs.

Garnish pork roast with baked garlic bulbs, sprigs of rosemary and halved fresh figs, in season or fresh plum or peach wedges. Serve with choice of vegetables and crusty Italian bread slices drizzled with olive oil.

Main Dishes

Veal Marsala

Ingredients

8 3-oz. veal cutlets, pounded
½ cup flour
½ tsp. dry basil
½ tsp. dry oregano
½ tsp. sea salt
¼ tsp. black pepper, fresh ground
2 tbsp. butter
2 tbsp. extra virgin olive oil
1 sprig rosemary, stem removed
4 cloves garlic, smashed
1 large shallot, green onion or small yellow onion, thinly sliced
8 oz. fresh mushrooms, quartered
1 tbsp. fresh basil, chopped
1 tbsp. fresh oregano leaves
¼ cup Marsala white wine
Pinch crushed red pepper
2 bay leaves

Directions

1. Place veal cutlets on a solid flat surface, and pound each with a kitchen mallet until noticeably thinner.

2. In a large zippered plastic bag, mix flour with dry oregano, dry basil, salt and pepper. Place cutlets, 2 at a time, in the bag and gently shake until lightly coated. Set aside for 10 minutes.

3. In a large skillet over medium-high heat, melt butter with olive oil and add rosemary, garlic, and shallot and simmer for 3 minutes.

4. Add veal cutlets, cook until lightly brown on both sides.

5. Add mushrooms, fresh basil and oregano and reduce heat to low and cook with cover for 10 minutes.

6. Pour in wine, dash of red pepper and let simmer for an additional 5 minutes to flavor and further tenderize the succulent veal.

Garnish with bay leaves. Serve with lightly toasted Italian bread slices sprinkled with parmesan to collect the sauce.

Main Dishes

Stuffed Bell Peppers

Ingredients

1 lb. ground beef

1 small yellow onion, chopped

1 rib celery, chopped

$1/2$ cup brown rice, cooked

6 large fresh bell peppers

1 cup of water

8 tbsp. extra virgin olive oil, divided

2 anchovy fillets dried and salted

14.5 oz. can diced tomatoes

6 tbsp. Aunt Margie's Prepared Breadcrumbs (page 34)

3 cloves of garlic, minced

1 tsp. fresh squeezed lemon juice

1 tbsp. fresh oregano leaves, cut

$1 1/2$ tbsp. fresh basil leaves, cut

$1/2$ tsp. sea salt

$1/4$ tsp. ground black pepper

$1/4$ tsp. crushed red pepper

Directions

1. Cook $1/2$ cup brown rice.

2. In a skillet over medium heat, sauté onions and celery in 2 tbsp. olive oil until translucent. Add ground beef and cook until evenly browned.

3. Rinse and dry the peppers. Slice the top of pepper off about $1/2$" down from shoulder. Remove and discard the seeds, hollowing out the peppers. Put the stem tops aside for later use. Spray olive oil on the bottom of a ceramic baking pan and stand peppers upright.

4. In a large bowl, mix the anchovies into 3 tbsp. of olive oil until mostly dissolved.

5. Add browned beef mixture, cooked rice, diced tomatoes, breadcrumbs, garlic, onion, celery, lemon juice, oregano, basil, salt, and pepper. Mix thoroughly.

6. Fill hollowed peppers with the mixture and replace the stem tops.

7. Drizzle the stuffed peppers with olive oil and bake at 350°F for 55 minutes until the peppers are tender.

Serve with pasta sauce topping and sesame bread sticks, or as a veggie side to a meat dish.

Main Dishes

71

Flaky Breaded Salmon

Ingredients

2 lb. salmon filet (works for any filet of fish), cut into individual serving size pieces

1 1/4 cups Aunt Margie's Prepared Breadcrumbs (page 34)

1 egg, beaten

4 tsp. extra virgin olive oil

1 lemon, cut into wedges

Fresh ground horseradish

Dash black pepper

Dash crushed red pepper

Directions

1. Preheat oven to 375°F.
2. Wash salmon filets under cold running water. Lightly pat dry with paper towels.
3. Place breadcrumbs on flat plate and beaten egg in a medium bowl.
4. Dip filets in egg and completely cover both sides with prepared breadcrumbs.
5. Spray a light coating of olive oil on the bottom of a baking dish and place breaded filets in a single layer. If salmon has skin, place skin-side down.
6. Spoon a light drizzle of virgin olive oil on filets and sprinkle with black pepper and crushed red pepper.
7. Bake at 375°F for 10-20 minutes, depending on thickness. Broil for 1-3 minutes, or until light golden brown. Test with fork, salmon should be flaky. Do not overcook.

Serve with lemon wedges, fresh ground horseradish and a side of black or brown rice.

Shrimp Scampi

Ingredients

1 1/2 lbs. uncooked medium shrimp
1/4 cup extra virgin olive oil
2 tsp. fresh oregano, chopped
1/4 cup fresh parsley, chopped
3 cloves fresh garlic, minced
1/8 cup parmesan or romano, grated
1/4 cup fresh squeezed lemon juice
1/4 tsp. sea salt
Dash black pepper
Dash crushed red pepper
1 fresh lemon, wedged

Directions

1. Clean and leave tail shell on uncooked shrimp.
2. Place shrimp in a single layer in a ceramic baking dish, leaving tails up and exposed.
3. Pour fresh lemon juice over shrimp and drizzle with olive oil.
4. Sprinkle with parmesan cheese, minced garlic, chopped oregano, half the chopped parsley, salt and black and crushed red pepper.
5. Bake at 425°F for 10-12 minutes.

Serve over linguine, fettuccine or angel hair pasta. Garnish with lemon wedges and a sprinkling of chopped parsley.

Linguine with Clam Sauce

Ingredients

1 lb. linguine

¼ cup extra virgin olive oil

3 cloves garlic, minced

1 tsp. dried thyme leaves

1 tbsp. of fresh basil, chopped

¼ cup Italian white wine

1 dozen large, fresh clams
 (discard if open) or
 2 7-oz. cans of chopped clams,
 with clam broth

½ tsp. black pepper, freshly ground

3 sprigs fresh parsley, chopped

4 tbsp. parmesan cheese, grated

Optional to taste:
6 filets flat anchovies, chopped

½ tsp. crushed red pepper

Directions

1. Under cold running water, rub fresh clams with small brush to clean. Bring a large pot of water with 1 tbsp. of olive oil and 1 tsp. sea salt to a boil. Add cleaned clams to boiling water for two minutes until clam meat is firm but not hard nor rubbery. Remove clams with a slotted spoon and let cool. Remove from shells and cut to 1/2" pieces. Set aside.

2. Slowly pour clam broth into large bowl, discarding sand from bottom of pot. Pour most of clam brothwater back into large pot and bring to a boil. Hold some clam broth for later.

3. Add linguine to boiling clam brothwater and cook for about 7 minutes, until al dente. The linguine will continue to cook in sauce later.

4. In a large skillet heated over medium heat, add extra virgin olive oil, garlic, thyme, and basil. Optional ingredients of anchovies and crushed red pepper can be added at this point.

5. Simmer together for 5-10 minutes. If cooking with anchovies, simmer until anchovies melt into oil and break up completely.

6. Add wine to the skillet and give a light stir.

7. Add clams and their broth. Sprinkle with fresh ground pepper and a pinch of chopped parsley.

8. Drain pasta and add it to the clam sauce.

9. Toss and stir for 2-3 minutes until the flavor of the clam sauce absorbs into the pasta.

10. Remove from heat.

Serve in a large bowl sprinkled with grated parmesan cheese and chopped parsley. Enjoy with a glass of Venetian Pinot Grigio.

Main Dishes

Spaghetti with Ricotta and Tomato

Ingredients

1 lb. spaghetti or fettuccine
6 tbsp. extra virgin olive oil
2 cloves garlic, smashed
1/2 tsp. sea salt
20 small tomatoes, (plum, cherry or grape tomatoes), halved or quartered
8 oz. ricotta cheese
2 tbsp. basil leaves, chopped
3 tbsp. parmesan cheese, grated
2 tbsp. Italian white wine
1/2 tsp. crushed red pepper
Dash of black pepper

Directions

1. Place pasta in boiling, salted water with a tbsp. of olive oil and cook for 7 minutes until al dente.

2. While the pasta cooks, heat 3 tbsp. of olive oil in a saucepan on medium heat.

3. Add garlic and sauté until golden brown.

4. Add salt and tomatoes and cook for 3 minutes.

5. Add ricotta cheese and 1 cup of the pasta water to saucepan and mix.

6. Add the drained pasta, grated parmesan cheese, wine and half the basil to the sauce and cook for no more than 1 additional minute.

Serve topped with fresh basil, black pepper, drizzle of olive oil, crushed red pepper to taste and a sprinkle of grated parmesan cheese.

Mussels in Wine Sauce

Ingredients

3 lbs. fresh mussels
5 tbsp. extra virgin olive oil
1 tbsp. butter
3 cloves garlic, minced
1 tsp. lemon juice
3 tbsp. fresh parsley, chopped
1/2 tsp. crushed red pepper
1 cup Italian red wine
1/2 tsp. sea salt
5 tbsp. red wine vinegar
Dash fresh black pepper

Directions

1. Clean mussels thoroughly by rinsing under water, removing sand and dirt, discarding mussels that are open.
2. In a large saucepan with lid, heat olive oil, butter and garlic on high heat until garlic is slightly brown.
3. Add lemon juice, most of the parsley, crushed red pepper and the mussels. Give the pan a stir and cook with lid on for a minute.
4. Cover the mussels with the wine and salt and simmer with lid on for 3-4 additional minutes (mussels should begin opening).
5. Add red wine vinegar and black pepper, remove lid and continue to cook 2-3 more minutes, until all mussels open.
6. Remove and discard mussels that remain closed.

Serve over pasta or with hard Italian bread slices to soak up sauces. Sprinkle with parsley.

Blue Claw Crab Sauce

Ingredients

6 live blue claw crabs
6 tbsp. extra virgin olive oil
3 cloves garlic, thinly sliced
½ tsp. sea salt
½ tsp. ground black pepper
2 28-oz. cans crushed tomatoes
1 tbsp. fresh basil leaves, cut
3 tbsp. fresh parsley, cut
4 medium bay leaves, whole
¼ cup burgundy wine
¼ tsp. crushed red pepper

Directions

1. With heavy rubber gloves on, thoroughly clean crabs under running water. Remove the top shell by pulling up on the flap on white bottom of crab. Remove the gills and discard along with the shell. Rinse the inside of the crab. You may be able to buy the fresh crabs de-shelled and cleaned. Or frozen.

2. Heat the olive oil in a large saucepan on medium heat and lightly brown the garlic, salt and pepper for 3 minutes.

3. Add the crushed tomatoes, basil, parsley, bay leaves, wine and red pepper and stir.

4. Place the crabs in the saucepan, cover and cook on medium heat for 1¼ hours, stirring occasionally.

5. Remove crabs from sauce and enjoy as a next course. A nutcracker will help crack the shells.

Serve crab sauce over linguine or fettuccine with a sprinkle of grated romano cheese. Serve crabs as a side dish with hard bread wedges.

Main Dishes

81

Fresh Spinach & Clams

Ingredients

12 oz. fresh spinach or
 16 oz. package frozen spinach
 or 14 oz. can leaf spinach

1 dozen fresh clams, steamed
 and chopped or a 7 oz. can
 chopped clams

3 tbsp. extra virgin olive oil

1 clove garlic, minced

1/4 tsp. garlic salt

Dash black pepper

Dash crushed red pepper

1/2 tsp. fresh lemon juice

1 tbsp. parmesan cheese, grated

Directions

1. Thoroughly clean fresh spinach and in a medium saucepan, bring the spinach to a quick boil in a cup of water, or heat frozen or canned spinach.

2. Drain most of the water and set aside.

3. Wash clams under cold running water. Discard if clams are open. Place in skillet with 1/2 cup of water on high heat. When water starts to boil, turn off heat, cover and let stand 5 minutes.

4. Remove clams from shell and chop into bite size pieces. Discard unopened clams.

5. Add clams, olive oil, garlic, garlic salt, black and red pepper and lemon juice to spinach. Mix well.

Sprinkle with grated parmesan cheese and serve.

Aunt Margie's Meatloaf Siciliano

Ingredients

½ cup extra virgin olive oil, divided

1 large onion, minced

3 cloves garlic, minced

⅓ cup burgundy wine

1 cup pasta sauce (page 42), divided

2 tsp. Worcestershire sauce, divided

1½ lbs. ground beef

½ lb. ground pork

⅔ cup Aunt Margie's Prepared Breadcrumbs (page 34)

⅔ cup romano cheese, grated

¼ cup fresh parsley, chopped

½ tsp. dried oregano

2 eggs, beaten

4 eggs, hard-boiled & peeled

Dash sea salt, black pepper and crushed red pepper

Directions

1. Preheat oven to 350°F.

2. Heat ¼ cup olive oil in skillet and sauté onion until golden and translucent. Add minced garlic and sauté for 1 minute. Remove from heat and blend in wine, ½ cup pasta sauce and 1½ tsp. Worcestershire sauce. Set aside to cool.

3. In a large bowl mix ground beef and ground pork, breadcrumbs, romano cheese, parsley, and oregano.

4. In a small bowl whisk 2 eggs, add dash of salt, black and red pepper, and add to meat mixture. When onion mixture has cooled, add to meat mixture and mix thoroughly with hands.

5. Divide mixture into 2 and spread 1 part into a greased baking loaf pan. Peel hardboiled eggs and lay them in a row down the middle. Shape the remaining mixture over the eggs, compressing it slightly to remove any air pockets.

6. In a small bowl, whisk ¼ cup olive oil, ½ tsp. Worcestershire sauce and ½ cup pasta sauce. Brush mixture over top of meatloaf.

7. Bake uncovered for 1 hour, 20 minutes, until the juices run clear. Do not over bake. Let sit for 15 minutes.

Garnish with parsley, slice and serve with roasted potatoes.

Desserts

Italian Almond Cookies	86
Fruit Filled Cookies	87
Aunt Margie's Cheese Cake	88
Chocolate Cream Roll	89
Millie's Rum Fruit Cake	90
Sour Cream Coffee Cake	91
Holiday Butter Cookies	92
Butter Almond Cookies	93
Easter Grain Ricotta Pie–Pizza Gran	94
Rum Raisin Cheese Cake	95
Italian Sesame Candy	96
Italian Honey Strips Pastry	97
Sesame Seed Cookies	98
Lemon Ricotta Cookies	99
Sfige–Sweet Ricotta Pastry Puffs	100
Zeppoli–Non-Sweet Ricotta Pastry Puffs	101
Chocolate Biscotti	102
Anise Biscotti Toast	103
Almond Chocolate Chunk Biscotti	104
Aunt Margie's Banana Bread	106
Almond Poppy Seed Muffins	107
Homemade Zesty Lemon Ice	108

Desserts

Italian Almond Cookies

Ingredients

2 eggs, whole
3/4 cup sugar
3/4 cup brown sugar
1/3 cup cooking oil
1/4 cup water
1 tsp. vanilla extract
3 1/4 cups flour
4 tsp. baking powder
1 tsp. ground cloves
1 1/2 tsp. ground cinnamon
2 tsp. ground nutmeg
2 tbsp. grated orange peel
2 cups whole almonds
1 egg white, whisked

Directions

1. In a large bowl beat both sugars with 2 whole eggs until smooth and creamy.
2. Add most of oil and beat until blended. Retain some oil to coat cookie sheet.
3. Mix water and vanilla extract into batter.
4. Blend in flour, baking powder, spices and orange peel.
5. Fold almonds into batter.
6. Coat large cookie sheet with remaining oil. Divide batter into 6 parts. Form each into a long 3" wide strip.
7. Place the 6 strips approx. 2" apart on cookie sheet.
8. Whisk the egg white in a small bowl and with a pastry brush, cover the tops of each strip with egg white.
9. Bake at 375°F for 30 minutes.
10. Remove from oven and let cool for 5 minutes.
11. When warm, cut the strips into 1" wide cookies with a sharp knife. Some breakage will occur.

Desserts

Fruit Filled Cookies

Ingredients

1/2 cup vegetable shortening
3/4 cup sugar
1 egg, beaten
1/2 tsp. lemon extract
2 tsp. baking powder
1/8 tsp. sea salt
1/4 cup milk
1 tsp. lemon zest
 (see page 108 for easy method)
2 1/2 cups flour

Fruit Filling

1 cup raisins, chopped
1 cup dates, chopped
1/3 cup walnuts, chopped
1/2 cup sugar
2 1/2 tsp. flour
1/4 cup water
1/2 cup grape juice

Directions

1. In a large bowl beat the shortening with the sugar until light and fluffy.

2. Add egg, beating well. Add lemon extract, baking powder and salt, alternating with the milk. Stir in the grated lemon zest.

3. Slowly add flour, mixing well until dough forms a ball.

4. Seal in plastic wrap and refrigerate for 30 minutes.

5. In a saucepan combine the ingredients for the filling. Mix well and cook for 10 minutes on medium heat. Continue simmering while slowly stirring until mixture becomes quite thick. Remove from heat, set aside.

6. Remove cookie dough from refrigerator. On a floured flat surface, roll dough to approximately 1/8" thick.

7. Cut dough into 3" circles. Place a tsp. of filling in center and fold in sides towards center, pinching 3 corners to shape a triangle, leaving filling area open.

8. Spray oil on a cookie sheet and place cookies 1" apart. Bake in preheated oven at 375°F for 15 minutes.

Aunt Margie's Cheese Cake

Ingredients

16 oz. cream cheese, 2 packages
2 eggs, beaten
1 cup sugar
1 heaping tablespoon cornstarch
1 tsp. vanilla extract
1 tsp. lemon juice
1 cup sour cream

Directions

1. Leave cream cheese at room temperature for 1-2 hours.
2. In a large bowl, combine eggs, sugar and cornstarch and beat until light and creamy.
3. Add softened cream cheese and mix in thoroughly.
4. Add vanilla, lemon juice and sour cream and mix well.
5. Pour batter into shortening greased and flour-dusted spring form baking pan.
6. Bake at 350°F for 45 minutes.
7. Turn oven off but leave the cheese cake in the oven with oven door open for 20 additional minutes.
8. Let sit for at least 30 minutes prior to serving.

Garnish with fresh sliced strawberries.

Chocolate Cream Roll

Ingredients

3/4 cup sugar
4 eggs, separated
6 tbsp. cake flour
6 tbsp. unsweetened cocoa
1 tsp. vanilla extract
1/2 tsp. baking powder
1/4 tsp. sea salt

Filling
1/4 cup powdered sugar
16 oz. heavy cream, whipped

Topping
1/4 cup powdered sugar

Directions

1. In a large bowl, beat 4 egg whites until stiff.
2. Slowly fold in 3/4 cup of sugar.
3. In a separate bowl, beat 4 egg yolks and vanilla.
4. Fold yolk mixture into egg white mixture.
5. In a medium bowl, mix dry ingredients until blended.
6. Add dry mixture 1/4 at a time, until blended smoothly.
7. Heat oven to 400°F.
8. Spray 10" x 14" cookie sheet with vegetable oil and pour in mixture. Flatten and even batter with rubber spatula or long knife.
9. Bake for 10-12 minutes. Do not dry out by overbaking.
10. Remove from pan and cool slightly.
11. Whip cream and powdered sugar together in small bowl until stiff peaks form. Spread whipped cream over cooled flat chocolate cake and gently roll up, starting from short end.
12. Place seam side down and lightly dust top with powdered sugar. Cut 1" wide circular slices.

Serve with fresh berries or peaches.

Millie's Rum Fruit Cake

Ingredients

4 oz. butter, 1 stick
1 cup water
1/2 cup dates
1/2 cup raisins
1/2 cup dried apricots, sliced
1/2 cup citron dry fruit
1/2 cup walnuts, chopped
1/2 tsp. ground cinnamon
1 tsp. baking soda
1 cup sugar
2 eggs, beaten
2 cups flour
1/8 cup rum
1/2 tsp. vanilla extract
2 tbsp. lemon juice

Directions

1. Soften butter at room temperature.
2. In a medium saucepan, bring water to a boil and add dates, raisins, apricots, citron, walnuts, cinnamon and baking soda. Remove from heat and set aside.
3. In a large bowl, mix butter and sugar until creamy. Gradually add eggs and beat until smooth.
4. Combine fruit mixture from saucepan with blended butter, sugar and eggs.
5. Mix in flour, rum, vanilla and lemon juice until smooth.
6. Pour batter into loaf baking pan coated with shortening.
7. Bake at 375°F for 40-45 minutes. Do not overbake as it will dry out and lose necessary moistness and flavor.

Top a slice with cream cheese and serve with espresso.

Sour Cream Coffee Cake

Ingredients

4 oz. butter, 1 stick
1 cup sugar
2 eggs, beaten
1 tsp. vanilla extract
1 tsp. baking powder
1 tsp. baking soda
1/4 tsp. sea salt
1 3/4 cups flour
1 cup sour cream

Filling & topping

1/4 cup sugar
1 tsp. ground cinnamon
1/2 tsp. ground cloves
1/2 tsp. ground nutmeg
1/2 cup walnuts, chopped
1/2 cup white raisins, chopped

Directions

1. Let butter stand at room temperature until soft.
2. In a large bowl, gradually blend sugar with butter until light and fluffy. Beat in eggs one at a time.
3. Add vanilla, salt, baking powder and soda. Mix well.
4. Mix in flour and sour cream and beat until smooth.
5. In a small bowl, mix filling and topping ingredients.
6. Coat bread loaf baking pan with shortening and pour 1/2 batter into pan and cover with nearly all the filling mix, leaving some for topping.
7. Add remaining batter and sprinkle with remaining filling/topping mix.
8. Bake at 350°F for 45 minutes, or less. Do not overbake. Test after 35 minutes with a toothpick in center. If toothpick comes out clean, it is done. If not, continue baking and testing every 5 minutes until done. Allow cake to cool.

Top with cream cheese and fruit preserves and serve with your favorite coffee or hot chocolate.

Holiday Butter Cookies

Ingredients

8 oz. butter, 2 sticks
1/2 cup powdered sugar
1 tsp. vanilla extract
2 1/4 cups flour

Directions

1. Soften butter at room temperature. In large bowl, mix butter with sugar and vanilla extract. Blend until smooth.
2. Add flour gradually, mixing well. Form into a ball and seal in plastic wrap. Refrigerate 1 hour.
3. Preheat oven to 375°F.
4. Place dough in a cookie press and squeeze out onto a cookie sheet. Do not grease pan.
5. Without cookie press, roll dough to 1/4" with rolling pin on floured flat surface and press out circle with a small juice glass. Place 1" apart on uncoated cookie sheet.
6. Bake 10 minutes, to light golden color. Do not overbake.

Decorate cookie tops prior to baking with cut pieces of maraschino cherries, spoonful of jam or chopped nuts. Decorate after baking, when cool with frosting and sprinkles.

Butter Almond Cookies

Ingredients

8 oz. butter, 2 sticks
1 cup powdered sugar
1 tsp. almond extract
1/2 tsp. vanilla extract
2 cups flour
1 cup almonds, finely chopped

Cream Cheese Glaze:

4 oz. cream cheese, softened
1/2 cup powdered sugar
1 tsp. vanilla extract
3-4 tbsp. milk

Directions

1. Soften butter at room temperature. In large mixing bowl, beat butter and sugar until smooth.
2. Add almond and vanilla extracts and mix in well.
3. Gradually add flour to mixture and work in almonds until batter is a dough-like consistency.
4. Shape batter into a ball and dust with flour. Seal in plastic wrap and refrigerate for at least 1 hour.
5. Preheat oven to 350°F.
6. With rolling pin, roll out cookie dough to 1/2" thick. With a cookie cutter, cut out star shaped cookies, or other cutter shape, and place 1" apart on uncoated cookie sheet.
7. Bake 18-20 minutes, careful not to overbake.
8. In a small bowl, mix glaze ingredients. When cookies cool to slightly warm, glaze tops.

Serve with demitasse, anisette and lemon twist.

Easter Grain Ricotta Pie – Pizza Gran

Ingredients

For the crust:

2 cups flour
2 tbsp. sugar
2 tsp. baking powder
Pinch of sea salt
1 oz. butter, ¼ stick
2 tbsp. vegetable shortening
2 eggs, lightly beaten
1 tsp. vanilla extract
3 tbsp. cold milk

Filling Ingredients

24 oz. ricotta cheese, drained
1 cup sugar
5 eggs
8 oz. dry whole wheat berries
½ tsp. ground cinnamon
¼ cup citron – dry fruit

Topping

1/4 cup powdered sugar

Directions

Pie Crust

1. In a large bowl, sift and blend flour, sugar, baking powder and salt.
2. Add the butter and shortening into the mixture using a pastry cutter or fork. Mix until crumbly.
3. Whisk eggs and vanilla together and add to the mixture.
4. Add milk and work the mixture with your hands to form a dough. Work just until the dough comes together.
5. Seal in plastic wrap and refrigerate for at least 1 hour.
6. Place cold dough on flat floured surface and using a rolling pin, roll the dough out to a thickness of ⅛". Fit and shape the dough into a spring form pan and refrigerate.
7. Preheat oven to 350°F

Pie Filling

1. In a medium bowl beat the ricotta cheese with the sugar.
2. Add eggs one at a time, beating well after each addition.
3. Boil and drain wheat berries and add along with cinnamon and citron. Stir to a smooth and even consistency.
4. Pour the filling into the refrigerated pan, top with pie crust strips and bake for 1 hour until golden brown.
5. Allow to cool. Sprinkle top with powdered sugar. Serve warm or chilled.

Pie wedges can be served topped with whipped cream or chocolate bits and your favorite hot beverage.

Rum Raisin Cheese Cake

Ingredients

6 tbsp. graham cracker crumbs

$1/8$ cup of white seedless raisins

$1/4$ cup of rum

24 oz. ricotta cheese

1 cup sugar

6 egg yokes

6 egg whites

$1/4$ cup flour

$1/2$ tsp. vanilla extract

1/2 cup sliced toasted almonds for garnish

Directions

1. Preheat oven to 425°F.

2. Coat 12-inch spring form pan with vegetable shortening and sprinkle bottom with graham cracker crumbs.

3. Soak raisins in rum until plump. Set aside.

4. In a large bowl beat ricotta with $1/2$ cup of sugar until smooth and well blended.

5. Add egg yolks one at a time and beat after each. Add flour and vanilla and beat until smooth.

6. In a separate bowl, beat the egg whites and remaining $1/2$ cup of sugar with an electric mixer on high until they hold peaks. Fold into the ricotta mix.

7. Add rum with raisins to batter.

8. Pour batter into prepared spring form pan and place pan on cookie sheet to catch spills.

9. Bake in preheated oven at 425°F for 10 minutes, then lower temperature to 350°F and continue to bake for 1 hour.

10. Turn off oven and allow cheese cake to gradually cool and set with oven door closed for approximately 3-4 hours.

Garnish with sliced almonds and serve with fruit compote.

Italian Sesame Candy

Ingredients

8 oz. honey

3 tbsp. sugar

1/2 cup sesame seeds

1/2 cup sliced almonds

Directions

1. Spray vegetable oil on 10" x 14" cookie pan and set aside.
2. Combine honey and sugar in saucepan and while stirring on low heat gradually bring to a boil.
3. Add sesame seeds and almonds to hot mix and continue to stir to blend well.
4. Pour hot candy mix onto the prepared cookie pan.
5. When almost cool slice with knife to 1/2" x 3" pieces.

Italian Honey Strips Pastry

Ingredients

3 cups flour
6 eggs, beaten
1 1/2 tsp. baking soda
1 tsp. sea salt
1 tsp. vanilla extract
1 tsp. ground cinnamon
2 cups vegetable cooking oil
8 oz. honey

Directions

1. Place flour in a large bowl.
2. In a medium bowl beat eggs.
3. Mix eggs gradually into flour until smooth.
4. Add baking soda, salt, vanilla extract and cinnamon to mixture and blend well.
5. Form dough into a ball, dust with flour and seal with plastic wrap. Place in refrigerator for 15-20 minutes.
6. With a rolling pin, roll dough to 1/8" and cut into 1" x 6" long strips. Twist strips into spiral shapes or tie like a pretzel.
7. In a large pot, heat oil until hot. Protect hands and face. Deep fry strips to a light golden brown, turning as needed. Place on paper towels to drain excess oil.
8. In a large skillet, heat honey on medium heat. Dip and cover pastry strips in honey and remove quickly.

Serve with sliced pears and espresso with anisette and lemon twist.

Sesame Seed Cookies

Ingredients

4 oz. butter, 1 stick
1/2 cup sugar
2 eggs, beaten
1 tsp. vanilla extract
2 cups flour
2 tsp. baking powder
Pinch of sea salt
1/4 cup milk
1 1/2 cups toasted sesame seeds

Directions

1. Let butter stand at room temperature until it softens.
2. In a large bowl combine butter and sugar until smooth.
3. Gradually add eggs and vanilla extract.
4. In a separate bowl, mix flour, baking powder and salt. Add to butter mixture and blend well.
5. Form dough into a ball, cover with plastic wrap and refrigerate for 30 minutes.
6. Roll to 1/8" thick, cut 1" wide strips and trim to 3" long.
7. Preheat oven to 350°F.
8. On flat pan, dip strips in milk and coat both sides by pressing and rolling over flat surface of sesame seeds.
9. Spray cookie sheet with vegetable oil spray and position cookies 1/2" apart on pan.
10. Bake 10-15 minutes, until golden brown.
Do not dry cookies out by overbaking.

Serve topped with a drizzle of melted chocolate bits and sliced strawberries.

Lemon Ricotta Cookies

Ingredients

2 1/2 cups flour
1 tsp. baking powder
1/2 tsp. sea salt
4 oz. butter, 1 stick
2 cups sugar
2 eggs
15 oz. ricotta cheese
3 tbsp. lemon juice
Zest of 1 lemon
 (see page 108, #2 for easy method)

Lemon Zest Glaze

1 1/2 cups powdered sugar
3 tbsp. lemon juice
Zest of 1 lemon

Directions

1. Let butter stand at room temperature until it softens.
2. In a medium bowl mix flour, baking powder and salt. Set aside.
3. In a large bowl, mix softened butter and sugar with an electric mixer until light and fluffy. Add eggs one at a time, beating until thoroughly blended.
4. Add ricotta cheese, lemon juice and zest. Beat until blended. Stir in the dry ingredients until smooth.
5. Prepare 2 cookie sheets by spraying with a light coating of vegetable oil. Preheat oven to 375°F.
6. Drop the cookie dough by spoonfuls on prepared cookie sheets, leaving 1" between cookies. Bake for 15 minutes, until edges are golden brown.
7. Remove from oven and let cookies cool on baking sheets for 20 minutes. Mix glaze ingredients together. Remove cookies from baking sheets and apply glaze with a pastry brush. When glaze hardens, refrigerate cookies in airtight container.

Sfinge—Sweet Ricotta Pastry Puffs

Ingredients

1 cup flour
15 oz. ricotta cheese
1/4 cup milk
2 eggs, beaten
1 tbsp. sugar
1 tsp. baking powder
1/2 tsp. vanilla extract
1/8 tsp. ground cinnamon
2 cups vegetable oil
1/4 cup powdered sugar

Directions

1. In a large bowl, mix and blend flour, ricotta, milk, eggs, sugar, baking powder, vanilla and cinnamon until batter is blended well and smooth. Cook just before serving.

2. Heat oil in deep saucepan to hot on medium heat–do not boil or burn oil. Protect yourself from hot splattering oil with eyewear, gloves and apron.

3. Drop batter one tablespoon at a time in hot oil and cook until golden brown, turning often with slotted spoon.

4. Drain excess oil on paper towels.

Serve warm with a sprinkle of powdered sugar.

Desserts

Zeppole — Non-Sweet Pastry Puffs

Ingredients

1 package dry yeast
1 cup warm water
1/8 tsp. sea salt
1/8 tsp. sugar
1 1/4 cups flour
2 cups vegetable oil

Directions

1. In a large bowl dissolve yeast, salt and sugar in warm water by stirring gently.

2. Blend in flour slowly and let stand for 15 minutes.

3. Sprinkle a light dusting of flour over the ball of dough, cover with a damp cloth and let rise for one hour in warm area.

4. Heat oil in deep saucepan to hot on medium heat–do not boil or burn oil. Protect yourself from hot splattering oil with eyewear, gloves and apron.

5. Drop batter one tablespoon at a time in hot oil and cook until golden brown, turning often with slotted spoon.

6. Drain excess oil on paper towels.

Serve warm with a sprinkle of coarse salt or cinnamon.

Chocolate Biscotti

Ingredients

1 1/2 cups of flour
3 egg whites
1/3 cup vegetable oil
3/4 cup sugar
1/2 cup unsweetened cocoa
2 tbsp. Italian black coffee
1 tsp. vanilla extract
1 tsp. baking powder
1/2 tsp. baking soda
1/3 cup sliced almonds
1/3 cup dried cherries
1 tbsp. anisette liquore

Directions

1. Preheat oven to 350°F.
2. In a large bowl, combine and mix all ingredients and beat to a smooth batter consistency.
3. Coat cookie sheet with vegetable shortening. Form dough-like batter into an oblong long loaf no higher than 1" at center.
4. Bake at 350°F for 20-30 minutes until golden brown.
5. While still warm, cut loaf into 1" wide strips, remove and stack on platter. Some breakage will occur.

Serve with fresh strawberries, pears and hot cocoa.

Anise Biscotti Toast

Ingredients

4 oz. butter, 1 stick
6 eggs
1 cup sugar
2 1/2 cups flour
1 tsp. vanilla extract
3 tsp. baking powder
4 drops anise oil extract
1 tsp. anisette liquore
1 tsp. anise seed
1/2 tsp. sea salt

Directions

1. Let butter soften at room temperature.
2. In a large bowl combine and mix all ingredients and beat to a smooth batter.
3. Coat cookie sheet with vegetable shortening. Form dough-like batter into an oblong long loaf no higher than 1" at center.
4. Bake at 350°F for 20-30 minutes until golden brown.
5. While still warm, cut loaf into 1" wide strips, and stack.

Serve with demitasse espresso, anisette and a twist of lemon peel.

Almond Chocolate Chunk Biscotti

Ingredients

1 1/2 cups whole almonds
2 cups flour
1/2 tsp. baking soda
1/2 tsp. baking powder
1/8 tsp. sea salt
2/3 cup sugar
1/4 cup dark brown sugar
1 cup semisweet chocolate chips
2 eggs
1 tsp. vanilla extract
1 tsp. almond extract
3 tbsp. amaretto liquore

Directions

1. Preheat oven to 350°F.

2. Spread the almonds on a cookie sheet and toast for 10-15 minutes, shaking pan a couple of times until almonds are a light golden brown. Empty onto a cool cookie sheet and set aside to cool completely.

3. Preheat oven to 375°F. Line 1 large or 2 small cookie sheets with aluminum foil, shiny side up.

4. In a large bowl, mix together flour, baking soda, baking powder, salt and both sugars. Place 2/3 cup of this mixture into a blender or food processor. Add 2/3 cup of the cooled toasted almonds and pulse blend until almonds are chopped.

5. Pour mixture back into the dry ingredients bowl.

6. Add the remaining almonds and chocolate chips. Stir.

7. In a small bowl, whisk the eggs, extracts and amaretto together. Stir into the dry ingredients until moistened.

8. Wet hands and continue working ingredients together until a dough forms. Divide the dough into 4 portions.

9. Mold each portion into a long oblong loaf, approximately 8" long x 3" wide x 1" high.

10. Place on cookie sheets leaving 2" between loaves.

11. Bake 25 minutes. If using 2 cookie sheets, reverse the position of pans in oven after 15 minutes.

12. Remove from oven and with a spatula and mitt, remove the loaves from foil and place on a cutting board to cool for 5 minutes. Reduce oven temperature to 275°F.

13. With a large sharp knife, cut the loaves into slices about 1/2–3/4" wide. Place the slices, cut side down, back onto cookie sheets. Some breakage will occur.

14. Re-bake biscotti at 275°F for 25-30 minutes.

15. With oven off and door slightly open, let biscotti cool. Store in an airtight container.

Serve with cappuccino or hot cocoa and fresh fruit slices.

Desserts

Aunt Margie's Banana Bread

Ingredients

4 oz. butter, 1 stick
8 oz. cream cheese, 1 pkg.
2 eggs, beaten
1 cup ripe bananas, mashed
1 tsp. vanilla extract
3 tbsp. sour cream
2 1/4 cups flour
1 1/4 cup sugar
1 1/2 tsp. baking powder
1/2 tsp. baking soda
2 tbsp. brown sugar
2 tsp. ground cinnamon
1/2 tsp. sea salt
3/4 cup chopped walnuts

Directions

1. Soften butter and cream cheese at room temperature.
2. Preheat oven to 350°F.
3. In a medium bowl, mix and blend softened butter and cream cheese with eggs, bananas, vanilla and sour cream.
4. In a large bowl, mix flour, both sugars, baking powder and soda, cinnamon, salt and walnuts. Make a well in the middle.
5. Add wet mixture into well of dry ingredients and blend. Do not overmix, some lumps should remain.
6. Coat loaf pan with shortening and pour in batter evenly.
7. Bake at 350°F for 40-45 minutes. Do not overbake, test after 35 minutes with toothpick–banana bread is done when toothpick comes out dry.

Serve warm slices with cream cheese and fruit preserves with coffee, tea or hot cocoa.

Almond Poppy Seed Muffins

Ingredients

1 egg, beaten
$1/3$ cup vegetable oil
$1/4$ cup of milk
$1/2$ cup sour cream
$1/2$ tsp. almond extract
$1\ 1/2$ cups flour
$1/2$ cup sugar
Pinch sea salt
$1/4$ tsp. ground cinnamon
$1/2$ tsp. baking powder
$1/4$ tsp. baking soda
$1/2$ cup almonds, sliced
2 tbsp. poppy seeds

Directions

1. In a medium bowl mix egg, vegetable oil, milk, sour cream and almond extract.

2. In a second bowl mix flour, sugar, salt, cinnamon, baking powder, baking soda, almost all of the almonds (hold some back for topping), and all the poppy seeds.

3. Make a well in the flour mixture and add liquid mixture and gently blend together until smooth. Store muffin batter in refrigerator overnight. Bake fresh to serve warm.

4. In a medium, 12-muffin baking pan, line with pleated baking cups or spray with cooking oil.

5. Fill cups $2/3$ full. Can sprinkle remaining almonds on top.

6. Bake in a preheated oven at 375°F for 15-18 minutes, until golden brown. Test with toothpick–muffins are done when toothpick comes out dry.

Serve warm with hot beverage. Delicious and aromatic.

Homemade Zesty Lemon Ice

Ingredients

6 large lemons
1 quart seltzer, sparkling water
3 tbsp. sugar
  (+ or – to taste)
1 tbsp. honey

Directions

1. Cut lemons in half. Rotate and squeeze over glass juicer. Eliminate seeds from juice.

2. Gently grate the outer rind with a cheese grater until fine lemony zest sticks to grater. Hold grater with grated lemon rind bits over a bowl and wash out rind pieces with water. Let pieces settle to bottom of bowl to retrieve later with spoon.

3. In a large bowl dissolve sugar and honey in seltzer and add the lemon juice and lemon zest bits. Mix together well. Pour into a freezer-safe container and place in freezer.

4. Scrape the mixture with a fork three or four times as it begins to freeze, to break it into ice crystals.

5. Scrape block of frozen lemon ice with a flat metal ice scraper to 'snow' the ice. Place lemon ice into a cup. Garnish with a thin lemon slice.

Cool, tasty and refreshing. Eat and enjoy!

Desserts

109